The Taste of Blood

poems by

Linda Lancione

Finishing Line Press
Georgetown, Kentucky

The Taste of Blood

Copyright © 2016 by Linda Lancione
ISBN 978-1-944899-23-3 First Edition
All rights reserved under International and Pan-American Copyright Conventions. No part of this book may be reproduced in any manner whatsoever without written permission from the publisher, except in the case of brief quotations embodied in critical articles and reviews.

ACKNOWLEDGMENTS

My thanks go to the editors of the following publications, where several of these poems first appeared or were honored:

Spillway: "Fish"
Aldebaran Review: "The Taste of Blood"
Pikeville Review: "Change of Heart," "Out of Silence" (earlier versions)
Changing Harm to Harmony, an anthology of poems about bullying published by the Marin Poetry Center: "This Isn't Happening" (as "Again")
Atlanta Review: International Merit Award for "Your Legacy," "The Taste of Blood"

I am grateful to Joan Houlihan and the Colrain Manuscript Conferences for an intensive education in putting together a manuscript and to the Montalvo Center for the Arts for a 2014 residency in the Lucas Artists Program, where this sequence of poems took shape.
Thanks also to Leah Maines and Finishing Line Press for their devotion to publishing poetry chapbooks and for their attention to my work.

Editor: Christen Kincaid

Cover Art: Linda Lancione

Author Photo: Nancy Rothstein Photography

Cover Design: Elizabeth Maines

Printed in the USA on acid-free paper.
Order online: www.finishinglinepress.com
  also available on amazon.com

Author inquiries and mail orders:
Finishing Line Press
P. O. Box 1626
Georgetown, Kentucky 40324
U. S. A.

Table of Contents

The Taste of Blood 1

Last Words 2

"Stormy Weather" 3

What Happened to Everything 4

The Help 5

No Mailbox 6

Your Legacy 7

How It Is 8

His Version 10

Trapped 11

Petition 12

Note to Dad 13

Snapshot, 1953 14

Note to Mom 15

This Isn't Happening 16

Change of Heart 17

You Come to Mine, I Come to Yours 18

"Lost Coast" 19

Unbound 20

Out of Silence 21

Anasazi 22

Fish 23

for the brothers—
Bill
Dad and Joe
Jason and John-David

THE TASTE OF BLOOD

We grew up in gardens, we grew up
with hammers lying around.
At a family barbeque, five years old,
I bit my brother on the shoulder,
he barely walking, younger
than my granddaughter.
I can still see those even teeth marks,
tiny square dents filling with red.
Then the fuss.
In fourth grade, Cheryl Young slept over
and we played with his little prick.
The next day, Mom moved his bed
into the dining room. How was that,
to camp out where they carved the turkey?
No wonder when they got old
he took over the whole house.
I want to see him again, my brother.
I want to cover his hands with mine
at least once before it's over.
But I'll never forget that wild joy,
sinking my teeth into his tender flesh.

LAST WORDS

You sneered
as I backed and turned my car
between your tool truck
and your tarp-covered lathe.
In a sweat, I leaned out the window and said,
"Next time, you might think
of pulling your truck forward,"
no doubt in my snottiest voice.

Finger-jabbing, spitting through your beard,
you yelled,
"You've got no right to ask me
for anything, get the fuck off the property,
stay away from my house."

Dad, dazed and scared,
stared out silent from his glider.
And what did *I* do?
I turned away
punched up the car window button,
nosed my Honda up the driveway,
and pulled out on the country road,
away from the house
that was new when I was,
where I stood on the front porch
before the lawn was even planted
wearing a bonnet and muff that matched,
still an only child, smiling.

Your house?

"STORMY WEATHER"

The day after your arrest,
as my car rolled down the driveway,
I saw, first thing, Dad's slashed-up old recliner,
its yellowed stuffing foaming over the lawn.
On the ground, my shoes crunched glass—
garage windows bullet-shattered.
In the kitchen, a legion of empty beer bottles,
a rank pot of raw chicken,
the freezer jammed full of old black phones.

But the living room? Tidy as a shrine.
Mom smiled from the sepia wedding photo
propped on the mantle, the piano lamp
beamed down on the sheet music of
her favorite song. You'd set out
a glued-together ceramic ashtray
just so on the polished coffee table
ready for the quiet, orderly man
you wanted to become.

WHAT HAPPENED TO EVERYTHING

I put your stuff in storage, all of it,
including the rented porn flicks.
Old pictures you liked—Grandma's tall
framed Yosemite Falls, the broken phones,
even the boards shot full of holes.

That two-ton tooling machine—
a lathe, I think—that stood for years
under a tarp in the driveway?
I paid a guy two hundred bucks
to haul it to the storage place by the highway.

Towed your tool truck (bad master cylinder)
to Uncle Hayden's, where it still sits,
wheels sunk in mud. Left your keys,
a change of clothes, your mail on the front seat.
Unopened last I checked. Our uncle's long dead.

Mom's violin everyone hoped was a Strad,
that you locked up in the basement?
Cracked from the cold. I showed an expert
the plaque inside—Cremona, Italy, 1679.
He asked if I always believed what I read.

Mom died first.
And, when you got locked up,
Dad sobbed at night.
Didn't think you'd ever get out.

The money from the house
I split down the middle, your account and mine,
according to their will.
But, what happened to everything?
You're the one I want to tell.

THE HELP

One by one they left, thanks to you.
You drove them away—the TV-watching
Ethiopians (last straw: you dumped a pot
of coffee over their just-cleaned stove)

and before that, Bible-toting Iris,
with her b.o. and brown dresses,
who got her old car up our long hill
on Jesus power.

Estrella, who cradled Mom on the couch
and could make Dad laugh with her teasing,
came back again and again, so loyal,
but one day when she woke to find

her green card and her clothes
smoldering in the fireplace
she told Dad, "Him or me,"
then quit for good.

Soon I, his own daughter,
had to say that too.
And Dad, of course, chose you.

NO MAILBOX

So you've become a total recluse,
up the north coast smoking dope
in that cold barn you built,
downing your lithium—or not.
I found your number on Anywho.com.
Why even *have* a phone?
I sure won't call, you'd
slam it down or swear at me or worse,
like years ago when you called to say
"Sorry I've been out of touch—been
on a secret mission, PT boat, captured,
held prisoner by the Japs."

Christ, what a story, in that war
you weren't even born. Yet I swear,
the regret in your voice was genuine.
Now your Christmas card—
that is, mine to you—comes back marked,
'No mail receptacle.'
I'm your sister, dammit.
When our parents said or did dumb stuff,
we rolled our eyes at each other. Only us.

YOUR LEGACY

Okay, let's talk about your guns,
the rifles with their polished stocks,
upright sentinels on the rack
in your basement lair,
the boxed pistols pearly on their velvet.
You know, my sons used to sneak down there
on holidays while Mom and I were busy with the bird.
Of course they weren't supposed to touch
but did—how resist the shine of the forbidden?
Years later, the older one admitted,
Grandpa caught him staring
through the crosshairs at his brother.

You were their bearded uncle
in cowboy boots and leather hat,
a gruff, kind, mountain man who came and went.
You surprised them with your knowledge of
the science giants: Tesla, Feynman, Freeman Dyson,
and your get-rich-quick inventions.
But one day your mind bent so far
you turned your hunting rifle on a sheriff's deputy.
Court-ordered to sell your guns, put on a list,
but we knew you could restock at gun shows, flea markets.
Now each mass shooting stops us—
someone's uncle, brother. . .

HOW IT IS

Mom thought
his reservist weekends caused it,
honor-guarding flag-draped coffins
off the planes at Travis.

It was 1971. I was
too busy shouting Ho Ho
Ho Chi Minh to honor
the returning dead or ask
what could have harmed my brother.

Mom was afraid
he'd end up somewhere all by himself,
outside, huddled under a blanket.
She begged me
to make sure that didn't happen.

At Thanksgiving,
our aunt says,
"Not to blame, of course,
but you were the one
who put him away."

I imagine this 'put him away'
passed along from cousin to cousin
but whenever I see them, they act
as if I'd never had a brother

nor they, a little cousin Davy,
hair slicked to one side,
two front teeth missing.

I have no brother,
nor he, a keeper.
This is how it is.

HIS VERSION

. . . and another thing,
she controlled the money.
When I needed cash for the folks' groceries,
I had to ask her for it.
She stole the middle out of my life.
Now I look like an old codger with dead eyes—
like Dad.
And she has the nerve
to send a picture of her grandkid
with a note about bygones.
No way I'll ever set foot in her house.
I'll just sit here in the woods
and eat my own bacon and eggs
on Christmas. I tell people
"I don't have a sister."
Even if they don't ask.

TRAPPED

All night in our parents' house, he paced, my brother,
naked, wild-eyed, shouting as he stacked
pots and pans along the kitchen floor, barricade

against who knows what? A renegade, a cavalcade?
Everything is falling in. I'm not the lynch pin,
the free lunch, the church of duty. I refuse.

I'll trade him in for a better model, say,
sleekly quiet in an Italian suit, slicked back hair,
diamond ring, a ready checkbook.

"You can't walk away from it, you can't."
That's Daddy, talking to himself, talking to me.
He who can no longer even drive.

PETITION

Before the hearing
the beefy bailiff, sentry
at the empty judge's bench,
scowls and shakes his head as I
hand my folded letter up to him.

I'm afraid of a release, I plead,
even a short sentence.
This could become a mayhem case
of *such a quiet man,*
so tender with his mother.

As I speak, my voice gets stronger.

The bailiff hesitates, caught between
the risk of rule-breaking and
the risk of someone getting hurt,
then reaches down and takes the paper
from my outstretched hand.

NOTE TO DAD

When things are humming along,
my garden growing,

I sense you smiling down
as if death rendered you harmless, approving.

Then I roll my eyes your way
at how things have turned out.

Your son, at his place in the woods,
sits in the sun,

a half gallon of Gallo parked at his feet
just like you and your father before you.

You know, he hasn't spoken to me in twenty years.
Like you and your own sister.

The two of you turned your backs on each other
all the way to the end.

SNAPSHOT 1953

He who couldn't swim, Dad,
lies sprawled in plaid pants
on a gravel beach by the river,
his face covered with newspaper.
Mom, in shorts—good legs, sweet smile—
poses on a mid-stream boulder
behind my four-year-old brother.

I capture them—mother, brother—
with my new Brownie camera
before he tumbles into ice cold water.
She slides in after him, heedless of scrapes,
hauls him to shore and wraps him in
the beach towel she jerks out from under me.
Her teeth are chattering, I note coldly,
already poised to save myself.

NOTE TO MOM

I saw his place today, high picket gate
wide open, a cheap canvas chair
and empty wine jug—sound familiar?—
parked in a sunny spot by the barnlike workshop
he built thirty years ago, its redwood planks
now weathered to a deep russet glow.

No truck, maybe he'd gone for breakfast
at the local café, or to pick up half a pound of nails.
I inched past, not daring to turn in his driveway,
but for miles, driving southward home,
I scanned faces in each passing pickup
for his shrubby beard, gone white.

Out of his range, breathing free,
I started singing in the car. At Stewart's Point,
I stopped for a Dove Bar—our old fave—
chocolate on chocolate, cold sweet comfort.
Your son has a life—I just wanted you to know.
Now, will you let me go?

THIS ISN'T HAPPENING

Mom and Dad are both alive.
Mom, still clear-minded, cooks dinner every night,
managing a sweet smile when I come in.
Dad sits at the table waiting to be served.
But my brother's the one in charge, the crazy
are always in charge, it's dangerous
to cross them, one jab of a clown elbow
and they're lost, or ruin everything.

At night I walk down the street past the communist's
bleak stucco house spiky with palm trees, past
the blue cottage where the lady had a nervous breakdown:
dark rooms, afghans. What's a nervous breakdown, Mama?
Halloween, we were scared to ring the doorbells
on their unlit porches—this was the fifties,
before my brother was first shackled,
before I had kids of my own.

Now a young man comes toward me in a fancy restaurant,
letting in a cold wind. I recognize him,
handsome as De Niro in his dark suit,
but the strange light in his eyes can only mean one thing.
I tell myself this isn't happening, I belong somewhere else.
His shoulders are coated with big wet leaves.
They hang down his arms like a loose cape
and scatter over the tables as he heads straight for me.

CHANGE OF HEART

One morning soon after they died,
still in my pajamas,
I sat down and wrote him a letter,
even-handed, fair, no grievance,
only facts. Then, taking a deep breath,
I added one last line,
asking him not to contact me till
he'd had a change of heart,
stopped blaming me for everything.
That felt right, left the door open a crack,
yet maybe sheltered me from his attacks.

I snugly sealed the envelope, got up to
make my bed and sweep.
We'd never been close, so
how much could this hurt?

Then I remembered at age five,
watching Mom sweep the kitchen floor,
he, unborn, a big balloon ready to pop
beneath the peplum of her blue faille skirt.

YOU COME TO MINE,
I COME TO YOURS

Remember how we shared a room
when we were little?—
I strung a rope down the middle.

Now you come in from the wild
bow over my casket
clutching Shasta daisies from the gas station,
great uncle, yet stranger to my grandchild.

Or, I enter the refrigerated room,
nod, "Yes, that's him,"
then in your honor raise a glass or two
in some backwater saloon.

"LOST COAST"

hot afternoon, I slip into a documentary
and fall into my brother's world,
the rivers he moved north for,
the Smith, Eel, Gualala, Navarro,
buying land between two of them, he said,
so he could have a foot in each

culture of campers and hipwaders, hippies
and geezers, feuders and flymakers,
one man speaks of a 60-pound steelhead
so much life in it, so much fight in it
thousands of them, we thought it would last forever

his wife: *we saw the sun rise on the dewy ferns*
next time we looked up,
it was almost dark

then smoking so much dope he went
crazy again, jail, now years later maybe
housed somewhere wearing an ankle-bracelet,
bitter, tamed, broken, I don't know—
the fish from those rivers
all but gone

UNBOUND

I run,
heart pumping, leaping free,

headed south along the cliffs,
saluting sea lions,
bad knee not hurting yet—

Can you
run like this, my brother, can you
get out of here?

I release you
like one of those thrashing fish
you once so loved to catch

I throw you back

OUT OF SILENCE

You might speak to me again
the way you do in dreams,
enter the room as if nothing had happened,
come toward me with an unreadable look.

You might say "let bygones be bygones"
and toast me with a cup of water.

You might lay your head on my shoulder
and I might hold you, briefly,
but still not trust you.

Or, the phone might ring, and someone
tell me you're dead, and everything
mine to dispose of.

I might drive by your poor house
on its country road, check
if your truck is parked there.

That's something I might
go out of my way to do, and then
head home and phone someone
just to say, "I drove by my brother's place."

ANASAZI

On a September road trip, I scramble down the path at Mesa Verde
beneath the thick lip of sandstone cliff
and stand before ancient dwellings,
rooms carved into pink rock open like a stage.

The guide speaks of dents in the earth
believed to be spirit holes
since Indian spirits dwell below like the mole.
From such a hole—*sipapu*—the first human was born.

> Today is your birthday.

A thousand years ago this tribe left to go south
leaving only the smoke-stained rocks from their fires.
No one knows why.
Now swallows dart in and out of their empty towers.

> And where are you, birth brother, blood brother,
> better loved when absent?

As spreading shadows erase the pearly light,
a breeze ruffles up with soothing news—
these people were my ancestors, not of blood, but of land.

I pry a stone loose from the ruins when no one's looking
and hurl it into the bottomless canyon.
I know I'll never hear it hit water.

But still, I listen.

FISH

She touches my glass earrings
and I say *fish* and she says *fish*
with wonder, enunciating.
Fish in Nana's ears, fish in the lake,
fish on her dinner plate,
hot from Dada's frying pan,
with a blue painted fish underneath.
My dad ate cod—*baccalà*—
on Christmas Eve, and took a *baccalà*—
a swat on the side of the head
whenever his father,
deep in homemade *vino rosso*,
got mad. I mostly received
a threatening scowl, raised hand,
don't get smart or I'll give you a . . .
This girl, everyone's darling,
presses close to my knees,
walks deliberately 'round my chair
to check first one fish, then the other,
then joyfully hurls herself against me
as if she can't believe her good luck.

Linda Lancione grew up in the Bay Area and was educated at the University of California, Berkeley. After living in Europe for several years, she returned to Northern California and taught English as a Second Language to immigrants and refugees while writing and raising a family. In the 1990s she co-wrote two travel guides with Burl Willes, *Undiscovered Islands of the Mediterranean* and *Undiscovered Islands of the U.S. and Canadian West Coast*.

Linda began writing poems in the early seventies, influenced by the voice-liberating pantheon of feminist poets such as Sharon Olds, Adrienne Rich, Susan Griffin, and Alta. During the eighties, she was a faithful participant in the Berkeley Poets Coop workshop, and she continues to benefit from the joyful and thoughtful all-day meetings of her longtime writing group. She has attended poetry workshops at Tassajara Zen Center with Jane Hirshfield, the Squaw Valley Writers Conference, and the Colrain Manuscript Conference. Her poems have been published widely in literary journals and anthologies, as well as in three chapbooks, *Wanting the Moon, This Short Season,* and *2% Organic, Poems from a West Marin Dairy Barn*.

Though her primary focus has been poetry, she has also studied narrative prose writing in intensive workshops with Tom Jenks and Carol Edgarian, editors of *Narrative*. She has also taken several fruitful classes with Andy Couturier, author of *Writing Open the Mind*. Her personal essay, "The Currency of Love," was awarded *New Letters*' prize for best essay in 2010 and subsequently given special mention in both *The Pushcart Prize* and *The Best American Essays*. The judge, David Shields, described it as "heartfelt, ruthless, and bristling with intelligence."

She has a novel in progress, *Hawk's Reach*.

www.ingramcontent.com/pod-product-compliance
Lightning Source LLC
Chambersburg PA
CBHW060227050426
42446CB00013B/3205